THROUGH THE CRACKS

Trent Busch

Cover Artist: Faye Altman
Photograph: James Carper

First Edition: 2022
Rs. 200/-

Cyberwit.net
HIG 45 Kaushambi Kunj, Kalindipuram
Allahabad - 211011 (U.P.) India
http://www.cyberwit.net
Tel: +(91) 9415091004
E-mail: info@cyberwit.net

Printed at Repro Books India Ltd.

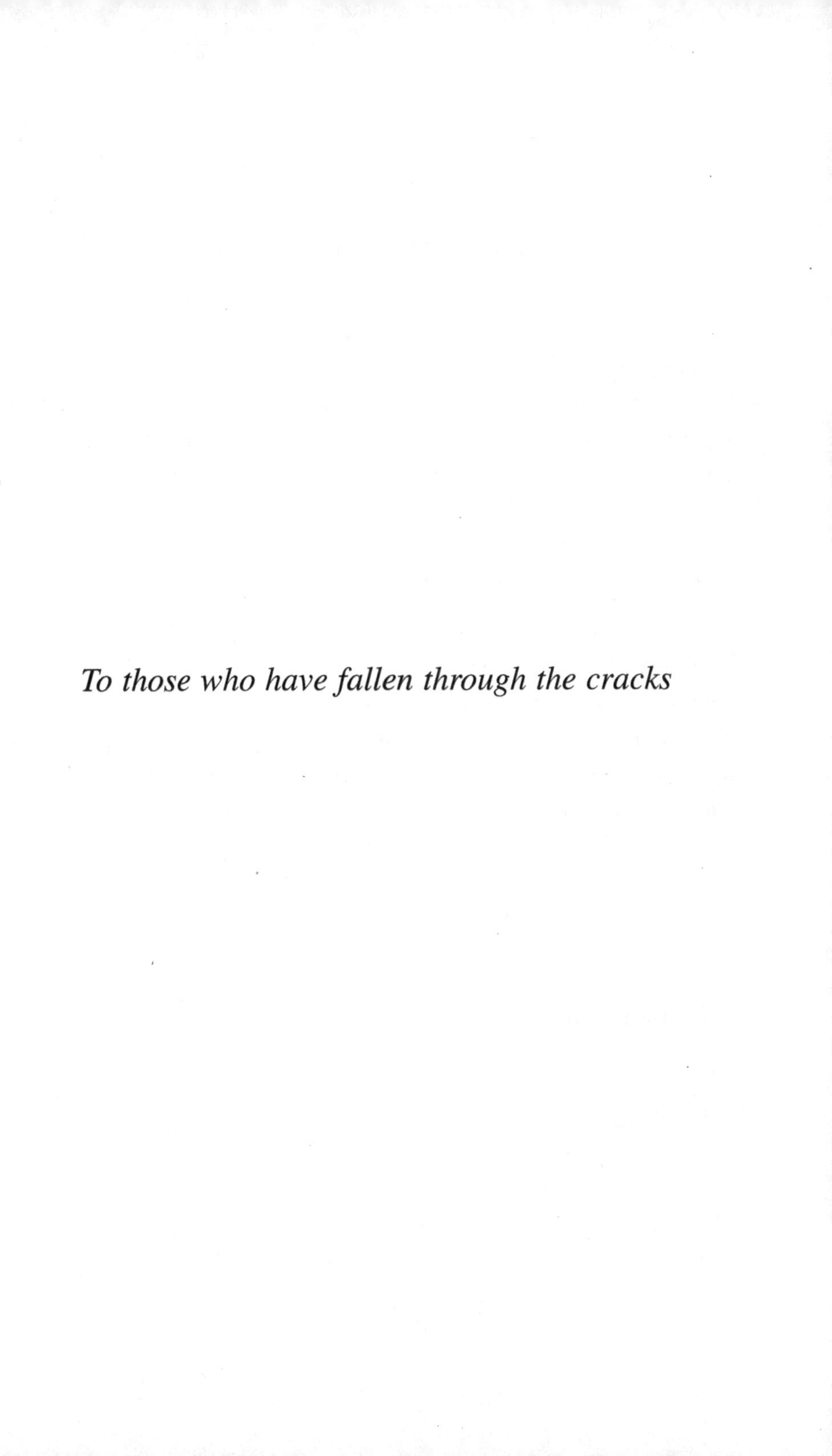

To those who have fallen through the cracks

AUTHOR'S NOTE

Although every poem in this book has been published* in a magazine or journal somewhere, none made it into one of my books. Somehow each one failed to become a member of a group, work itself into a section's sequence, or compliment the poem before or after it; in short, each time I tried to use it, it fell through the cracks and never found a place to belong. Finally, I thought why not toss them all out there with each other, without much help from me, and see what they come up with; that is, without rhyme or reason, let them fall where they would.

The result is this book. Of course, they found that the last thing you get to know is what comes first, and though they wander around a bit, the poems drift and glide to the places we see. Out of the young they have come, out of uncles and aunts, out of summers and winters, and out of the conversations at both home and on the road about all the daily parts we play that make us think about the things that are the best we ever saw. They have no noble aspirations: they do not try to establish values, improve virtue, or urge holy mysteries. Perhaps they fell into the places they knew they wanted to go.

Trent Busch

*There is one exception. "Aunt Hughie" still awaits her page.

ACKNOWLEDGEMENTS

Thanks to the editors of the following publications where poems, sometimes with different titles and in different form, first appeared.

The Alaska Quarterly Review, "Finally as the Wind"

The Appalachian Journal, "The Man and the Road"

Anemone, "Vonda Hays"

Anterior Review, "Safety in Dark Places"

Argestes, "Goff House"

Blue Buildings, "Glorious to Find an Uncle"

The Chaffin Review, "Persephone in New York"

Charleston Gazette Mail, "Hartley School"

Chiron Review, "Bear"

Cider Press Review, "Soft Rain through an Open Window" and "Personal"

The Cincinnati Poetry Review, "The Waiting"

Clockwatch Review, "The Orchard"

Cold Mountain Review, "Lucy Snyder"

The Comstock Review, "Playing Parts"

Connecticut Poetry Review, "Hands"

Crazyhorse, "Shelter"

Eclipse, "Jennifer Passing Through"

Epiphany, "The Unbroken"

Georgetown Review, "Burning the Letter"

The Georgia Review, "Statues"

Grasslands Review, "The Meadow's Edge"

Great River Review, "The Pantomime"

Habersham Review, "If the Branch Is Bare"

Harpur Palate, "Tactics"

HeartWood Literary Magazine, "Past the Millenium"

Hermeneutic Chaos Literary Journal, "At the Restaurant" and "The Keepers"

Interim, "This Day"

International Poetry Review, "Forget Horses" and "Lookout Point"

The Louisville Review, "The Door" and "A Story"

Mad Poet's Review, "House Payments"

Manhattan Poetry Review, "The Lost"

Memphis State Review, "Woman Leaving Beech Valley"

Missing Spoke, "Something Pretty"

The Ohio Journal, "Mail Pouch Curry"

Outerbridge, "Gaunt Ships"

Oyez Review, "Sophia"

Owen Wister Review, "When I Touched your Arm"

Paper Street, "Old Movies and a New Novel"

Poetry East, "Wild Seed"

Pen, "Spring Shoeing"

Quality American Poetry, "It Comes Rising Up"

Rainbow Curve, "The Photographs of Others"

Reed Magazine, "Quails"

Silk Road, "No Second Ending"

Snowy Egret, "Character" and "Haunted"

Southern Humanities Review, "Ceres without Persephone"

Subnivean, "The Cleaning Rod"

Third Coast, "Lines"

West Branch, "The Hero"

Widener Review, "The Touch"

Worcester Review, "Shadows along the Street"

The Woven Tale Press, "The Best you Ever Saw"

Writer's Forum, "Uncle Ace"

Xavier Review, "In the Old Field"

Contents

1 Young

HANDS

With one match
I light
the fatwood kindling;

smoke rolls
toward the night sky,
thick, in spirals,

as from some legendary
Engine #9 whistling
toward Baltimore.

In the leaping hands
we seem to discover
mystery of flame,

touch sparked by
heart in a zone
of brain millions

of years beyond
reptilian passion;
how one hand

leaves consciousness
cold, another starts
a quick burning.
How this difference

is our distinction,
our hands of affection,

used first to climb
down from trees
to these fires.

SOFT RAIN THROUGH AN OPEN WINDOW

What I know today is no more
than what I knew at ten,
clouds in a blue sky, until
language comes to explain:

so it is the image that
starts words, the way the rising
of the sun awakens a house
and puts the coffee on.

What I knew then was streaks
in a hillside dawn, soft rain
through an open window,
that for every bird that fell

there was a sleight of hand.
What I see today is a ridge
and a boy below a tree.
A crow flaps low toward

the night. What he believes
comes from the image that
he sees or the image
someone, his mother say,

has seen and changed to mean,
as clouds are seen, as these
words came to be: image
of a boy beneath a tree.

THE PHOTOGRAPHS OF OTHERS

We look at the youth in the picture
and see a person we can't believe,
the eyes without shadows, the rouged mouth,
the worried look or the happy look, young—

yet that somebody, that silence
from another time about to speak,
about to say, Catch me here, catch
this half-smile that I may never die,

is us where even the leaves across
the street in the background are waving,
a look belying intelligence
or crush on the homecoming queen.

It's the same in the photographs
of others where we try to be
more objective, not look away
so fast for fear of vanity,

providing us a carelessness
that permits a sterner look free
from tears, that youth can be understood
only when it is gone, that our lives

had a number of ways to go,
yet went this one. When we look off
this way, alone, we lock out voices
except the one that can never

speak, that young mouth saying, I fear
neither happiness nor sadness
nor the weight of tomorrow nor this
moment which can say nothing again.

THE TOUCH

The June day begins. I
walk across the square, smile
at another crossing there.
Quietly she smiles at me.

We have our work to do,
as others who have risen
by the clock to drive or walk
to where the world resumes.

The day is hot. We do
not stare at anything
for long. The windows tell
us that our lives are fair.

Once in a dream, or in
a dream I thought I had,
I saw a woman dressed
in white crossing a square.

Across, she stopped to stare
into the window of
a shop, then looked up and
touched my face in the glass.

Remembering, I put my hand
upon her hand that held
my face within the glass.
Again, I see that dress.

O lady in white, white
romance, to you who flood
the day with magic and lend
chance to our step, I make

this wish: that in the night,
smiles gone and faces off
and with long hand dredging
the dark, see us still as fair.

VONDA HAYS

All night I heard
their voices and his,
the man I was to marry,
begging Vonda, Vonda,

and once when he cried
upon God to please
fetch me back I nearly
went down to him.

But now it is over.
The sun has been
two hours in the sky
and I wait for a man

with wild hair
who talked me to hide
on this ledge which only
an eagle could find,

a drinking man,
a married man,
a man with words
full of honey

whose voice
is a ghost's
that can rally
the timid to dic.

I kneel here
in my broken shoes
and torn gown and think
of the altar I left,

the house that will
never be mine,
knowing when he comes
I will go, saying,

Oh, Jack Jack Jack!
oh, Jesus God,
what have I done
with my life.

AT THE RESTAURANT

"Who was it said, 'When there
is no light, think dark'"? "No
one," you said, the flattest
answer I ever heard.

When the dish is broken,
when the log has burned, when
the receiver at the
other end goes dead for

the last time, it is that
conversation echoes
the turn to whatever
will make us pretend that

nothing has happened, all
is well. Else, the fragile
ego, bare, raw to the
infectious day, knows

nothing to do but scream
and hide in Bedlam woods.
I thought you had not one
feeling, looking away.

I have forgotten what
old task I turned to then;
the waiter came and I
paid. Your back, as you left

before me, stopped all that
was behind you. I thought
of you in the street outside
as worn and solitary.

IF THE BRANCH IS BARE

Usually the directions
we go get us nowhere
in particular, whether
we take the red flashy
model or the brown Ford.

"My dad wanted me to
be a doctor" we never
get over, and "If I
had only" switches us
to the eyes of a daisy
in a lost field.

When we seem finally
to be going that straight
line for our mothers, it
is only that like the ball
of chance that clicks in
the casinos, we have

settled randomly on
a number and are old
enough to ride. The point
is there is no point for
most of us to center:
we exchange one set for

another, launching out
from this slot like the worn

caterpillar where
if the branch is bare, the
purse is rounded, never
dreaming of the butterfly.

It Comes Rising Up

In a red dress
thin as mist
on the sunrise field
you appeared
for a moment
to my sight
and I kissed you
O how
on the waiting mouth

and I felt you die,
and I died,
and grandmothers
died like dominoes
from Shreveport
to Savannah

and all along the 32nd
a delicious shadow
fell upon
the land of suntans.

BURNING THE LETTER

Before she burned it in
a silver tray, here as
if yesterday written
and delivered, she reread

the letter, summoning
still the fingers slender
and long that worked the words
to their certain meaning.

Then she thought of the child
she had been, he had been,
children of her own bred
with that tired mimicry,

how he had cried to have
her and not having her
because he cried, both had
turned remorseless shoulders

that in a moment might
have been forgiven had
the playthings of hours been
as permanent as hearts.

Watching it until flame
neared her fingers, she dropped
it in the silver tray,
pretending here no better

understanding than on
that day when she first read
it and wept and wondered
from where, where might joy come.

THE DOOR

The young woman came
to a door. She knocked.
An old man answered.
He wore a black coat
with dandruff on the
shoulders. Are you the
man I am looking for,
she said. Go to
Dever's Fork, he said.

She did. She came
to another door. She
knocked. The same old
man answered. Are
you looking for me,
she said. Go to
Twin Forks, he said.

When she came to
Twin Forks, the old man
was lying in a ditch.
He was dead. Some
dandruff jumped from
his coat onto her dress.

Oh, no, she said. She
ran to another door.
She knocked. Come in,
a voice said. Is this

the place, she said.
Yes, said the voice.
But you must hurry.
Powder your face and
change your dress. You
must not be recognized.

A young man came to the
door. He knocked. An
old woman answered. She
wore a black dress with
dandruff on her sleeves.
Are you the woman I am
looking for, he said.

A STORY

The man's face in the
window was handsome.

I tried not to follow.
No, I said. You want
me to jump off a cliff,
you want me to fall
down a well.

I tried not to go.
He led me to a cliff.
Jump off, he said.
But I would not.

He led me to a well.
Fall in, he said.
But I would not.

He led me to a river.
Trees leaned on the bank,
stars danced on the water.

All girls like to swim,
he said. Jump in.

I took off my clothes
and jumped in. The
water was warm. I swam
on my back. I floated
and went under.

Did you drown, he said.
And I had not.
Do you want to cry,
he said. And I did not.

Get dressed, he said.
I will help you
tell this story.

THE WAITING

I roll a cigarette
and stare
through the window
as the sun's
shadow
reaches the cliff
of the eastern hill.

The white porcelain
of the stove
and hanging pots
begins to fade
as night settles
in the room.

The first time
she did not come
I chopped wood
until I splintered
the handle of my ax.

The second time
I only
walked the room.

A man lives a little
at a time,
as a cigarette burns,
as the sun goes down.

She has brought
a strange stillness
to these hills.

NO SECOND ENDING

Sometimes I do not want to talk,
she said. Sometimes I know no one
but myself and by myself know
everybody else, which leads to error.

You, you have the salesman in you,
can talk to any strangers, sell them
a truck, a lake, a ticket to
a foreign place not on their map.

And make it stick. I do not call
you charlatan. Not a con man.
Not a bad man, yet who makes us
see it in ourselves what we lack.

Sometimes what I want is to be
a single daisy in a field
and be mistaken yet believe
all flowers have to share is chance.

I see you nod your head. I see
your willingness to agree that
eyes a light shade of blue might be
green. Oh, I see you smile good things.

You want sea shells on a beach, you
want a hundred boxes neatly stacked,
endings fixed, and in the end agree
to disagree without a twist.

WOMAN LEAVING BEECH VALLEY

Clouds are riding,
coming in quick
off the mountains.

I cross the bottom
in a rented car.
It is dusk and wind
at the window
makes my eyes water
like a caring mother.

Morning, snow will
have iced the ledge
of every banister.
Where it will hide
me I do not know:

I am one who is
lost forever, the
preacher says, if
I leave my husband.

Well, if it is so.
I have no reason,
complaint, or lover
but I know that
what makes a coward
is not a happy room.

I love this valley.
Guilt sweeps me like
a broom, but surely
there is a song
in me, a chance
waiting somewhere to
join a woman's hand.

Wind howls down, snow
begins, and I would
turn quickly home if
only I feared more the
night and storm than
what I leave behind.

THE MEADOW'S EDGE

We stood on the ridge road
and watched the morning fog
and the imagined ship
that passed us, going south.

When it sailed over pines
toward Big Springs you turned
and ignored the wet grass
of the meadow's edge, walking

back to the gray sedan
where you sat and stared at
anything that was not
me or us or the day.

No ship we ever saw
had the same crew or port,
I thought and stood and knew
not how to speak to you.

After that day we never
met again, turning off
the ridge and following
what I have now forgotten.

We were both right then. I
wonder now how you saw
that day, and if face to
face we might smile at our

ignorance of each other,
the way two animals meet
and sniff and turn away,
indifferent to destination.

2 ANCESTRAL

THE MAN AND THE ROAD

The road was there
and he used it,
walking through the country
of green trees
and long-stemmed flowers,
pausing to speak
to nesting birds
and box turtles.

One day he came
to a gap that led
to a field of mown grass;
he entered and saw
that the grass
was drying into hay.
He sat down.

A road is not a life,
he thought; it needs
a basket of chicken
and a jar of iced tea.

He stayed all day.
When the moon rose
white over the road
rabbits danced in the field
and took no notice of him.

He felt himself beginning
to disappear. First
his nose, then his cheeks
and hands. Finally, unable
to feel himself at all,
he vanished.

When the sun rose
over the woods
to cure the hay,
the grass he sat on
would not dry.

It did not cure,
as if a cloud
had taken it upon itself
to block the sun
and leave a dark circle
on the ground.

MAIL POUCH CURRY

His teeth are yellow.
Every day his sister
tells him to
clean up his mouth.

Once he did. Once
he brushed his teeth,
smiled at himself
in the looking glass,
and went to see
Ollie Anne Benson.

She let him kiss her.
He fell in love.
He put water on
his hair and took
her wild flowers.

She held onto his
arm. She told him
his bad habits.

She said tobacco breath
smelled like fox piss.
She said they
should get married.

He said he thought
they were. She said no.
He said he was late.

He likes his sister.
She cooks for him.
He says one woman
in a house is enough
to stay and keep
a mirror in her room.

GOFF HOUSE

Against the sky
house
of broken panes,
skeletal box.

We knew all
the families:
sometimes
two a year,
hanging clothes
in the wind,

children
peeping at doors,
vanishing
like small birds
at our approach.

The last, Goffs,
give the house
its name,
though no more
their house than
the dozen before.

No one's home,
stopping us to
say, Where have
they gone

that served
so constantly?

Reminding us
of all our houses,
against the time
even gods
must cry treason.

THE ORCHARD

Peaches have had their fling;
now is the time apples
ripen, and bent limbs of
pears burden the orchard.

My father, nearly blind,
standing by the window
shows us the scrape on his hand
and wants to know why skin
in old age gets rotten.

Mother says that that is
no way for him to talk
in the kitchen and hands
him a bucket to get
some fruit for breakfast.

She says he has begun
to talk that way lately,
which was never like him,
and his children should
visit him more often.

I go outside to help,
though I am not needed,
the day fair as all of
them seem to be when I
remember: the crates,

the market, the dark hair
on my father's arms as
he secured the ladders.

What should we say to each
other? He is that man
no longer? I am not
the boy on his shoulders
stretching for the highest fruit?

Now workers tend the trees.
We both know I could have
stayed if I had wanted,
his urging me to town
a guise for stubbornness.

The sun blooms full, making
boughs shadow each other,
the pear trees like heavy
mothers, as my father,
hidden, takes their fruit,
gentle with the shaking limbs.

GLORIOUS TO FIND AN UNCLE

Glorious to find an uncle
you knew only briefly
as a boy who once
quit three jobs in one
week during the depression
and later got caught
in another man's bedroom,
a scar across his
left sideburn that took
thirty-seven stitches
to prove it, and who
at last left his own
wife and several kids
to work on construction
five years in Roswell,
New Mexico,
          who now lives
on a farm, raises cattle,
and collects old-west pistols
and rifles and tells about
ten-gauge shotguns that used
to protect stagecoaches
and killed how-many Indians,
and explains to you in so many
nothings at all where
part of your blood came from.

AUNT HUGHIE

Seeing her sitting in a worn
coat on cold mornings, blowing
steam from her coffee, we watch
her stare out the window

at a hunched bird settled on
the light wire outsider our
building, guessing her talent
when she was Miss State Fair:

did she in a tight sweater
sing an old Clooney song
or in shorts send high into
the air magic batons?

We watch and look away
and watch again, trying
to remember when she forgot
her days, when her interest

in questions dimmed, answers
dressed in buttoned collars, purse
missing when she went shopping,
gestures coming without hands.

Again, we watch, an aunt we
know by photographs now taken
from her, unable to coax from
memory what the pictures say.

PAST THE MILLENNIUM

Nothing has come around the house
this morning I wasn't expecting,
the wren's quick song a false alarm;

still, winter's first snow on the lawn
quite surprises me, and I recall Hardy's
thrush announcing a new century.

To think it over a hundred years
ago he leaned upon his thicket gate
in woe far different from our own.

Could I, I would say to him, now
fully targeted as his Tennyson,
We still look up and give a start—

if sometimes from the fifteenth floor
on tubes you wouldn't understand—
at the moon's full gaze upon our art.

And add, could he listen, the bird's song
I heard today still sounds its promise;
the century's gate's as it was then.

HARTLEY SCHOOL

Six of us
in the eighth grade,
desks lined
below the windows
along the one-room wall:
Janice, John, Jake,
Vidella and Imogene.

Eight years of sitting,
the room
became a common home.

Gray winters with sledding
and forts of snow,
drying gloves
around the center stove—
softball in the fall
and spring.

Learned to live
with each other,
hated and loved,
promised and vowed;

for years, have not
kissed a cheek
or touched an arm:

none of us stayed
to make a living
from our land.

THE LOST

The wish to have back someone lost.
Sitting at the breakfast table
with husband or wife or pulling
the gate inward to pass into
the street, suddenly through the door

or stepping from behind an elm,
arms extended, your dead daughter
or Uncle Charley or the one
on whose breast you cried all night for
guilt or grief or feverish love.

For this reason we have romantic
comedies, novels, and Shakespeare,
even if we never linger
much upon the sequel, the cloyed
days, the spiritless hangovers.

The wish strung up with memory,
the lights upon a Christmas tree,
the star that when the tree is down
we wrap carefully in soft paper
to store away in our longing minds.

UNCLE ACE

Dead with the children,
though they are only dead
by distance, funeral visit away,
the heavy wife is lowered
beneath the blue canopy.

He will walk home, he says, not
far up the hollow to the ridge,
once their only road to town.
The daughters do not argue.

Home the eaves drip: clothes
to box for her sister;
mementos—the deal dresser
scattered with stick pins,
amber bottles, earrings and beads
he moved fifty years around
that will not adjust to his hands—
to put into a trunk and store away.

He touches the striped-back chair,
sees in the mirror the quilted
bed and clock, curses lowly
as hard thoughts skirt his brain,
threatening like horned angels:

a woman never pretty, just available,
a vessel for the throbbings
of an average man; how many nights

did he watch her flannelled back
until his own hungers died?

a woman with a barking voice,
whose shapeless presence
made him glad to eat alone,
whose ferret hands searched out
his whiskey, breaking bottles
against the corner stones
until he gave up drinking too;

a sick woman who would not die,
who ate the syrups, drank the pills,
lay the bed, weeping he did
not care for her and never was
the husband other women had.

But the angels only flirt. He has
knocked one like a wasp against
her picture with the two daughters.
Outside, night settles on the silent
house, eaves fill with darkened
water, the winter rain sets in.

WHEN I TOUCHED YOUR ARM

Your cry in the night was
not the cry of death—
only, perhaps, the fear
of hurt for your child

or cry for some long ago
love who, standing on
your front steps, looking at
his hands as if he

held a hat, said he was
not coming back, feeling
again the pain in his
voice and then your pain.

When I touched your arm, I
felt the calmness return
as it did to Juliet
learning that mere Tybalt

was slain, yet crying
out again when she found
Romeo gone. I had
tried to return calm,

as one who offers
a balloon to a child
whose kite's string is all
that's left in her hand.

What made me think then
that kindness and guilt
are one, the child repulsed
by solution, your cry

growing, as if my hand,
not arrived in time,
signaled some wrong I had
made, some dark I had done?

IN THE OLD FIELD

In the old field
stones
no one has overturned
for years:

under one
a two-story house,
porch gone,
now storing hay,

another,
a pregnant girl
wondering what
will she do,

and another,
dogs bringing
the cows home
at evening.

First,
it is pines
that thicket
years.

Hardwoods follow
and grouse
and deer
take cover.

Then, fathers
forbidden,
the stones
disappear.

THE HERO

The gate is locked.
The long lawn ends
in white columns.
I shake the bars.
You bitch, I say.
You high-rent bitch.

She comes to a window
and opens it. Throw
him into the road,
Charles, she says.

Charles wears a chauffeur's
hat and black boots.
Run along, sir, he says.
Madam is taking a nap.
Let's have no trouble.

I pretend to leave.
Charles falls asleep
under an apple tree. I
climb the fence and go
to her room. The door
is not locked but I
kick it down anyway.

She pulls a sheet
to her bosom. A horn
grows from each

temple and a ring
hangs from her nose.

I want my cow back,
I say. And my hog.
You are taking our farm
one head at a time.

Animal, she says. Get
out of my house.
She calls for Charles.
Charles comes. Some
violence without sex.

Charles groans in a
corner. She kneels
naked in front of me.
I tear the horns from
her temples. I rip
the ring from her nose.

I go back to my farm.
My wife runs to meet
me. The cow and hog
join us. We all laugh
happily and walk side by
side in the barnyard.

LINES

There is the smoothness
of the round rock
beaten by rain,

the slickness of sides
on the green
cube of candy.

This love is for you,
she said.
It is a stack of letters
tied with old ribbon.

There is the octagonal
cut of crystal,
the silver eye,

the honing of knives
on Arkansas stone,
steel shavings.

May death be
a smile of surprise,
she said,
the deftness of whiskey.

Stalls
in a scrubbed dairy,
egg in the straw.

SPRING SHOEING

In the shade of a pig-nut tree,
Flabby-armed Uncle Lead shod Prince.
He did resemble Vulcan, *mon oncle,*
Though he had no twisted sinews in his leg.

As son of Earth and Sky,
I served as assistant,
My part to say nothing
(To horse or man)
As I passed the nails.

One by one the four legs
Swung between my uncle's.
Rasping smoothed off broken edges;
Methodical hammering clinched
The square nails in a round row
On the rim of the hoof.

"How it must hurt him."
I flinched and squinted my eye
At each of his dull blows.
I was the only one who blinked.

Square nails, dead hoofs, flabby arms
Made Prince ready to pull the blunted plow
Round and round in our rocky garden.

3 Seasons

BEAR

From the barn he could see
the black bear in three seasons:
spring with cubs when it had
his mother's careful eyes;

in summer, his father,
wallowing the treetops
and leaving the rail fence
sprawling among the firs;

autumn, his favorite,
he saw himself stand to
listen and watch the sun
falling behind hills.

No thought of winter;
snow columned, he dreamed
the bear ripping the wolf
of seasons, his lineage,

the heart's deep roar, flick
of the short ear, moving,
if retreating, toward
the white and last frontier.

GAUNT SHIPS

The orange that in the morning sky
triggers the mind triggers mine; I
walk again in the cold hollow,
leaves down, where the bare cave beckons.

There on that morning, wind down with
no hope of rising, stripped to her
waist, Iphigcnia, bound and
held by her father's soldiers, waits.

While in another town, cushioned,
shouldering a gathered gown, fed
and pampered by a dozen arms,
Helen, hair up and blond, greets Paris.

The nature of the day does not
change; we must be the character
we own, the one we have been born
and groomed to play since Pisa.

Mostly our trips to Troy are on
the gaunt ships of the Greeks as we
look out at the red dawn, sailing on,
willing to afford whatever wind.

FINALLY AS THE WIND

"What good is sound without
thought," she said. "You are not
vulnerable to me
anymore." Closed the door
as finally as the wind.

And standing there before
the large window, he watched
her back the car into
the street, turn the wheel,
pull into another life.

From here we cannot see
where she disappeared, the route
she took, what change of face
she chose to take to stop
somewhere and change again.

Or know what she meant. Did
he one evening, reading
a newspaper or book
give some vital question an
impossible response,

or fail to fear the threat
that tore her voice when she
said, "and a mind still, and
dresses which on other
men are not always lost"?

So we stop here on this
image of her gone, left
only with the profile
of a man in a room
grown suddenly too small.

LOOKOUT POINT

A rotten way the leaves turned,
down in two showers:
no color at all
left the world.

Why was he crying?
What did I do
to a man who had
power-fisted his way
past sheet metalist
to foreman?

A child here,
a child there,
and suddenly
five flowering heads
eating cereal.

Whip him hard, Mommy,
whip him hard,
the cat's
in the washer
and his feet
are all muddy.

Just after nightfall,
just after the wind
has died in the
trees and the house
is empty—tomorrow.

Around daily
the day goes round
my spinning head
and damn it
to hell and all
the leaves (Christ
without mercy)
fell rotten this year.

HAUNTED

for Kendall and David

A sewing machine stops us
in one corner, rusted wheel
and slanted pedal, braced
halfway to turning under.

No hands for sewing:
vines, windows broken,
the sagging wallpaper
not even housing roaches.

We conjecture: what laced
maiden was once called
to supper, or the parlor,
where a red-wristed caller
stammered a proposal?

Or what woman stood to
curtains to watch children
move away, then sat as
someone told a final dying?

A parting question: who
would steal where everything
is stolen? The house lost;
better roof and walls
fall a rotting sepulcher.

We leave, our eyes
evasive with surmisings,
turning our conversation
to the yellow poplars, the
clay road past the cemetery
where someone last spring
saw the tracks of bear.

FORGET HORSES

A feeling you know
is the way
to describe mountains:

a cabin with high
porch stones
and two front windows
will do,

or a buck nosing
gently in the leaves,
then rubbing
his antlers
against a sapling.

Forget horses
unless you have ridden
the flight
of mountain lions
under the afternoon
of a whistling hawk.

Cypress will
not shade with spruce
and no
dialect is ever true,

but if streams rush
free and trout

are native,
drink the water.

A feeling you know:
the way a mountain
storm grows
when you wish
a mountain storm.

HOUSE PAYMENTS

The lawn hides a thousand
absurdities: pinchers,
feelers, white bands across
the backs of munching thieves,

the sun in lengthy league
with the rain and their hot
and cold subordinates
prying apart the boards

of walls and floors, warping
shingles and scaling paint
until maintenance is
a synonym for hunger.

Doors and windows have their
host of begging strangers
who wait all day for knocks
to be answered, dropping

from lintels, hurrying
with their spare luggage
around corners to safety
behind appliances.

Money is secondary;
your son's broken heart
and daughter's first period
teach the price of faces

paralyzed by a day
plainly ordinary
as the snake's skin they find
by the walk teaches them

the snake's price for growing.
You know next year will bring
more excessive spending;
you balance stubs and wait.

THE UNBROKEN

Then the time when anything
that's old loses resiliency,
begins to shake and wobble, sags
in most conspicuous places.

Old house for example (never
does a new house rattle windows)
that creaks like an old man walking
the winter fields after fodder.

Or the motor in the basement,
(gravel of bearings, straining
pulleys, the cracked belts threatening)
uneven in its promises.

We usually hear these sounds at
night or on a dry afternoon
when the sun is low, dust hanging
in red light, children moved away.

In time live on hope, the crooked
spindle right itself, foundation
settle true, and never despair
the unbroken; never, never.

THE PANTOMIME

He stood at a barn.
Darkness had fallen.
He felt something touch
his left shoulder
and looked back
to see Venus burning.

I will sleep here,
he said. He opened
the long doors
and climbed to
the mow. He lay
down on the hay.

I will hide from
her, he said. I
will cover my eyes
and not listen.

Through a crack in
the roof a woman
did a pantomime in
the sky. She stood
on one foot and lit
stars with her fingers.

She spoke to him
through the crack in
the roof. I have come

for you, she said. You
must rise and follow.

But I am bedded
for the night,
he said. I am
happy with the mice.
Come, she said. You
have been chosen.

She led him down
hollows. She took him
to slopes and caves
and put his hands
in strange apertures.
She made him rear and
rut like a stallion.

At daylight he was
lost between ridges.
He called to her
for direction but
she had disappeared
into the sky.

He heard hounds tracking.
The teeth, he said.
I must study moss.
He wet his finger
and ran into the wind.

She did not save him.
The hounds tongued

and caught him. They
left rags on his bones.

She bronzed the hounds'
heads. She gave them
human eyes. She
placed them in the
sky and every night
lit them like stars.

QUAILS

When the quails went up
in one flourish, he
felt his shoulders chill.

The big gun said boom
and down came feathers
all on the hillside.

When the bed was made
for the last time, they
do not recall it

for they were no more
than birds, yet who at
what age cannot be?

It was the hunting
season after all;
nowhere is protest.

Now, snow collects in
the oak's pockets. For
an hour it was fall.

SHADOWS ALONG THE STREET

 Some things need putting off:
the dread of going back
to work the second day
of a two-week vacation,

the cost of your daughter's
wedding when all she wants
is a swing ride at the city
park or a guest at tea.

Some things need forgotten:
the ring you were caught stealing
at Macy's, math tests,
the death of your first dog.

Still, there are things in
shadows along the street
we walk every day we
cannot put off until

next Tuesday, things farther
away but nearer, earth's
place in its circle of
the sun, your daughter's wedding.

Say what we see: that trees
confined to concrete squares
on busy streets or those
free to bend with others

in the park know when to
face the wind and drop their
leaves and the need to husk
their seeds for winter snow.

THIS DAY

Down the meadow where the heavy
tufts of grass hold the sides
of creek a woman sits, watching
minnows where the water
has cut a bend in the red bank.

Water runs deeper there and worn
stones have made a levee
that protects the bar where sprigs of
grass make futile start,
over which water does not flow.

She will remember this day, warm
sun, lazy sky, even
the color of dress and way her
feet swung out and over,
never quite reaching the water.

This day that mocks mourning,
the tall soldier who came
in his bright buttons to
a house that no matter
how prepared is never ready.

Somewhere, if you listen hard, you
can hear her story, how
her feet swung over the water,
how with years of wearing
the dress retains its soft gold.

WILD SEED

He had waited long enough and it
had repeated itself; after
months of doing something else, it
stood so close he could hear its breath.

What he did about it was what
he always did: follow its lead
to the sand and sugar cliff where
he descended into its camp,

regretting already what he
could not stop, what someone every
year wrote books about, what others
had done before the thought of books.

No one knew better than he the trap,
the wild seed in his mouth, tasting
nothing, the beckoning hand that
left him once more undone, alone

and waiting as that same hand took
off its glove to go underground
again, to point and clip and paste,
to brush its dying mother's hair.

SOMETHING PRETTY

How can I know what you
will be ten years from now?
Waking here to what you are,
seeing the base of hill,

the bare fruit trees, the white
cocoon on an outside
corner of your house, holding
that beautiful something

you know now is never
coming out. The path with
its unlucky turns which
would surely get no worse.

I know I did not help,
though we had our days, you
will say, that made biting
the inside of your mouth

easier. I could have
helped you list the other,
the lies that nights before
help us close our eyes to.

I did not. How can I
know? Looking back is to
see mistakes; memory
is easy we both learned.

I will give you something
pretty: woman in a scarf
bent at a woodpile on
a porch, standing up, face

cut with hurt, eyes toward
a seashore in the South,
saying, O you son of a bitch,
O you sweet son of a bitch.

JENNIFER PASSING THROUGH

The language that I speak
doesn't come from me
but through someone
else's voice;
                if I say
I love or hate you,
believe what you please.
I didn't say these things.

They're musings from one
looking out a window
urgent for fantasy
or romance,
                who imagines
us, trying to make
the words we would never
say easy to believe.

So if I walked all
day yesterday trying
to find a way to hold
your face,
                remember
he'll do anything
to shine up shoes
and start a dance.

What I feel is nothing
he's felt, what I've

done is nothing he's
seen,
    however true
it may seem to him;
I'm only as willing
or unwilling as he says.

4 Playing Parts

PLAYING PARTS

Being hero or villain,
walking down the slab steps
overwhelmed by the stench
into the labyrinth
of the Minotaur, that is
what we like.
        Sitting on
the bed's edge, our ankle
on our knee, tying
the shoe of the period,
our escort still undressed,
back turned and asleep,
pistol under the pillow.

So we say, playing parts
well in a world that is,
yet is not, make believe,
careful at shops, or in car
windows not to reveal
our secrets:
        the note kept
deep in our pockets, Rhett
on the stairs, Ariadne
abandoned on the rocks,
the long last look (we are
coming back) that says we
are never coming back.

STATUES

"I don't want to be drunk.
I don't want to be sober,"
young Jack Webb says
in the late movie.
"And pretty women bore me."

My friend and I can't get drunk.

Jack Webb, actor,
but someone wrote his lines,
and I say,
"Maybe what we ought to do
is sledge on a rock gang,
have someone lash us
with a black whip
when we don't pound—
maybe we'd appreciate."

"All I want is to find
out what I want," he says.

"Or to find the old west
again, maybe," I say.
"Dig up Doc Holliday,
live by him till
six tin cans will sail
off the dead tree into the arroyo
before the smoke clears."

"A highwayman would be
all right with me," he says.
"Not to know how much
money you'll get
or how much life is left—
a thing to live for."

A can in mid-air stops spinning,
a flapping jacket trails bronzed
above the frozen horse.
Doc Holliday smiles;
he is considering playing
Hieronimo in *The Spanish Tragedy*.

CERES WITHOUT PROSERPINE

Without mental stamina to
complete the farm, a shrine
to Ceres. Though his arms
are willows, his legs oaks,
design shatters, blueprint in
a hurricane, rafters raised,
sills lowered to no end.

Masterpiece skeleton of no
flesh, fields ragged with
rotting grain, imagined dog
bringing home no cow,
rat deserting to the river.

To wonder at in strength or
in desire: the sudden lack
of mind to lift design above
the earth to its completeness.
His shrine meant for goddess,
for plow and sowing,
for daughter he must
lose and find, son to touch
from death and teach the man.

The mind scatters, helpless
to conclude, as timbers mold
and wind razes the bony dream,
a ruin, if noticed, beyond even
conjecture by the passerby.

PERSEPHONE IN NEW YORK

The walls do not, but seem
to, move; we need not place
one ear upon the ground
to know the two lights of
the subway train;
                loaded
into its zoom, we swing
across the underworld;
mostly here the moods are
temperate, baggage light.

And do not think of those
days west, hard talk and weeks
of dust, trunks and bruised
breasts, the lye in the white
pantaloons;
            as they did not
think of an older world
that springs back to us:
released from hell on earth
to blink in that bright sun.

CHARACTER

You read at first
curiously about his
faded eyes and
four-day-old stubble,

then gain interest
when you notice
his soiled suspenders
and the dried tobacco
juice in the corner
of his mouth,

at last learning that
he runs a still and
sells red liquor in
quart jars like a man
who was killed in the
hollow above your house
when you were a boy,

and though he is from
Tennessee and you
live in West Virginia
suddenly your eyes
glaze and you say,

Oh, yes. My God, yes.
Yes, I know that man.

LUCY SNYDER

She ran into the forest,
white arms, white legs,
up hollows, across knobs,
the trees wailing.

She became a man with
a spike driven through
his eye. She held
her face, stumbling,
tripping over logs.

She became a woman
with a hatchet buried
in her skull. She
clutched at the handle,
leaping down a cliff,
running up a stream.

When she reached a
dark pool she tried
to scrub the white
from her arms and legs
but it spread to her
breasts and thighs.

She screamed, then went
under, thrashing
against a man's hands
penning her in a car.

Rangers wrapped her in
a blanket, parents
buried her on a ridge,
and a white rain washed
small gullies in the
clay of the red hills.

SHELTER

The story was not about
a dog, but a dog was its hero:
how on the one hand it was
a bitch and mated with every
breed on the block,

                     and on the other
a Bruno that dug its way
out from under whatever fence.

And so you read, Well, why does
Lady stay when she knows what he'll do?
Or, You tell me what I'll feel
when the others speak of their Rex
at the kennel;

                can I take the streets'
emptiness, a house over my head
and biscuit tins in the pantry?

The hero could have been a horse,
a frost, a train, still water,
but not have been women naked
as water or men furious
as axes;

          it was a story
not of midnight or noon, an all
day story, oblique with its wounds.

THE KEEPERS

There are those who know that
not everyone should be
allowed to touch their dress
or uniform; some know why.

But not all: those greedily
guarding it behind glass,
then at home walking out
as neighborhood enforcers,

others of self-importance
who think all hands are
attached to jam-eating
primates ready for pillage.

Our best keepers know the dead
have no need for their ware,
however much it was once
prized or worn thin living.

How passion must take form
in those invisible spirits,
or in us for them, when one holding
limp shoulders across an arm

traces the buttons with true
fingers to fashion again
victory or anguish, the letter
now answered and received.

TACTICS

Fitzgerald said he wrote
out of the authority of failure
and Hemingway
out of the authority of success.
Most understand the former,
as the topic illustrates,
but "the authority of success"?
The way Dickey wrote *Deliverance*?

Both succeeded, I suppose,
if we say the cheetah succeeds
after nine or ten tries
at tripping the gazelle
or the grizzly succeeds,
snatching a salmon in midair.

Can examples that tell us more
by indirection mask the door
we wreck into in the dark
or the sudden face we look up to
from tightening a screw into glass?

Fitzgerald knew best how to fail;
we understand that. But what he meant
about success, not counting luck,
we stumble at, and doubt
not because we don't believe it so
but from failing yet to see art
in gauzy dress or the old aficionado
take the double-barrel from his mouth.

SAFETY IN DARK PLACES

When an idea we held close
once, a hand-in-hand companion,
grows up, becomes distant, and moves
away, we lose not so much a friend

as confidence, the way a snake
cast from its skin does not see
the same world, seeking safety in
the darkest places, untested,

as we await what we hope will
be sharper focus, more grounded
in the way light balances, even
in shadow, what our wits can do.

Still, it is a loss of seasons,
the way the lights in our parents'
houses change over the years when
we drive up at dusk and find ourselves

strangers, as if what is lost for
what is new gives us a stricter
look as we sit quietly at first,
fearing what they and we will find.

OLD MOVIES AND A NEW NOVEL

Talking along this way to you
I never feel foolish, at least
not like the woman caught standing
crying to herself before her

bathroom mirror or the man in
his garage blowing on his
finger cursing the hammer he
has just thrown into the corner.

Yet there are times when what I say
makes me blush, such as "away she went
forever" or "not looking back,"
such things you know cannot be true.

What makes us say these things is not
true either, just human, the way
we want our lives to be scenes from
old movies and a new novel.

So as I talk along this way
to you, I think of the condor
riding invisible currents,
the foal being nudged to its feet

by its mother, if not human
things, the way we make them human,
as if forever happening,
as if they will always happen.

SOPHIA

Maybe if we look at her long
enough, we can know her case, if
we give her and ourselves time, for
we're in her life now as she's in ours.

It didn't take long to get involved
though she'll never see us, never
be affected in any way by our
interest, if not our concern.

Not exactly not our concern:
though we'll never give her money
or take her hand, we see in her
a window, reflecting what's there.

One thing we cannot miss is the way
she stays to herself, perfectly
happy now that whatever was
is over, pulling on soft gloves

in winter and in summer not
afraid to show her hands again,
even if she has no garden
and no longer prefers the light.

What we learn from her we remember
a long time, some things for the rest
of our lives or, rather, as long as they
can matter or we think they do.

It is an honest distance for
seeing, not hearing her wording,
the way she's caught turning, fingers
lightly holding the back of a chair.

THE BEST YOU EVER SAW

You go back to what it was like
years ago when words tumbled out
like desire for someone you could
not have, happening often then.

You talked and talked as if words were
what mouths were made for, filling rooms
with nonsense about signs and dreams,
the best actress you ever saw.

Now it's what you hope not to say
that eases what you are from corners
of rooms as you move and sit trying
not to startle, especially yourself.

And when you slip, a holiday
evening drinking with friends, voice
escaped surely not your own, you
swap silence for unintended probity,

then try to take it back, as if able to
be governed by will, wolf-hungry
need for words, the tree that loses
itself to the thunderstorm.

PERSONAL

When I open a door
I turn the knob gently,
fling it with my hand
or pull it wide, then look
inside before I enter.

The surprises waiting to
leap out red-eyed I learned
early from my father
when air was full of autumn
and oil field meter houses.

Caution dies hard, so if
you say to me, "Let's ride
over to White Pine and go
swimming" or "Send us
a batch by late October,"

know that my suspicion
at your offered hand
is my way to reckon
with those who say, "Oh, it
will be worth your while."

When I open a door
I do so with foreboding,
having seen the crouched feet
on door jambs, the fisted
head cocked above the floor.

THE CLEANING ROD

Had he had something else to do
that afternoon he would not have made
the cleaning rod for my .20 gauge,
whittled from basswood, straight as
arrows you could buy in town, pull
tapered and chamfered, the bottom
slot rounded for a polishing cloth.

He had a brother Lee Wires knew,
a grown daughter, but it was the wife
no one talked about, the ground not
turned for boys who must imagine
a lover, or her watching alone
at windows or sitting down to
a set table long ago cold.

Had he had something else to do
he might not have lingered, turning
his back almost as he handed
out a treasure, not interested
in gratitude, as if caught up
in the memory of a moment
he thought he had forgotten.

Until now, I don't remember
seeing him again clearly, shadows
that spoke and passed on store porch steps,
home of his gift and a token that
has stood silent in a gun not fired
in thirty years, hushing gossip,
closing that loud mouth like a bond.